GETTING UP FROM BEING DOWN

WORKBOOK

GETTING UP FROM BEING DOWN

WORKBOOK

STAND UP | REACH HIGH | FINISH STRONG

S. TODD TOWNSEND

Published by Redemption Press, PO Box 427, Enumclaw, WA 98022

Toll-free (844) 2REDEEM (273-3336)

Redemption Press is honored to present this title in partnership with the author. The views expressed or implied in this work are those of the author. Redemption Press provides our imprint seal representing design excellence, creative content, and high-quality production.

Unless otherwise indicated, Scripture verses are taken from the *New American Standard Bible*, © Copyright 1960, 1962, 1963, 1968, 1971, 1973, 1975, 1977, 1995 by the Lockman Foundation. Used by permission.

Scripture quotations marked KJV are taken from the Holy Bible, King James Version, © 1979, 1980, 1982 by Thomas Nelson, Inc., Publishers. Used by permission.

ISBN 13: 978-1-68314-782-4 (Paperback)

Library of Congress Catalog Card Number: 2018933295

Contents

Acknowledgments

THERE ARE A NUMBER OF people who helped forge the shape of this workbook and make it a reality. However, there is one person I wish to express special thanks and recognition to: Inger Logelin, Redemption Press senior editor, without whom this workbook would not exist. I almost canceled the idea, thinking the primary *Getting Up from Being Down* book would be enough. But once again, Inger provided exceptional coaching, counsel, editing, design, and a heightened literary standard to its completion. Her ideas and guidance have brought this workbook to life, and I am certain it will help others to accomplish their goals in life as they work through this workbook and find themselves . . . getting up from being down.

Introduction

MY TIME ON EARTH HAS had a thread running through it of *getting back up in life*. Does yours?

In the Word of God, there's a core message of hope, a holy thread of God's truth that weaves through the dark chapters of life. It's all about how you can get back up no matter how far you've fallen or how badly you've messed up.

This six-week workbook with five daily lessons each week is based on my book *Getting Up from Being Down*. We will explore questions on how to get up from a down lifestyle, how to endure, how to get up by believing and serving, and getting up and staying up.

How to Use This Workbook

1. Enjoy this workbook on your own. The book can be used as a daily devotional as each chapter is self-contained. For more enrichment, reread the designated chapters in *Getting Up from Being Down*. There are six weeks, each with five days of daily thoughts and questions for you to explore.

2. Or find another person or a small group to partner with for expanded discussion, prayer, and encouragement.

> Getting back up is the power God's given you to transform your life.

Nowhere But Up

He rose up! He's comin' back.
Now I'm a winner; it's like that.
HE ROSE FIRST, AND WE GOT THE VICTORY.
RESURRECTION IS THE WILL OF GOD FOR ME.

(Refer to chapter 1 in *Getting Up from Being Down*, "The Get-Back-Up Hook.")

AS ONE WHO WEARS MANY hats—pastor, lecturing professor, conference speaker, group fitness instructor, and author, to name a few—communicating and successfully getting my point across is important. I love building people up. I love motivating others to stand up, reach high, and finish strong. To that end, I'm always working to develop better personal techniques and more effective methods of communicating truth.

I also wear the hat of a rapper. As a rapper, I am moved by the way powerful truth is communicated with the help of syncopated beats, rhythm, and repetition. In a rap song, the hook—a short riff or phrase—is the catchiest part of the tune. Getting back up is a built-in hook in our lives. We are built by God to get back up. When we get back up, God transforms us spiritually after a failure or a fall.

We all fall down. All of us.

Have you ever seen a baby learning to walk? He takes a few steps, then loses his balance and falls down. What if the baby just gave up as if he were saying, "I just can't do it. I can't learn to walk"? What if he never tried to walk again? That would be ridiculous, wouldn't it?

Life offers us many opportunities to fall. But when we fall or fail in life, embarrassment, criticism, and fear of failure often keep us down.

Our call from God is to get up. It's always an *upward* call.

When we see a baby learning to walk and he wobbles and falls, we don't shame him, but encourage him to try again.

Has that been your experience when you have fallen?

Describe a time when you were just starting out in your Christian walk and you tried something new, failed, and then felt embarrassed by not doing it "right," or you felt awkward when you compared yourself to others. How did this affect your desire to step out, contribute, or share afterward?

_____

_____

_____

Perhaps your fall was a moral failure, a fall that had great consequences in your life and in your family's life. How did you get past that failure? Were you encouraged to get up again and start walking straight?

_____

_____

_____

Read 1 Corinthians 13:11: "When I was a child, I used to speak like a child, think like a child, reason like a child; when I became a man, I did away with childish things." Part of putting away childish things is getting up and trying again.

Do you give yourself permission to try new things and fail? Or do you give up after you fail and then don't try again?

Has there been something in your life that you have never tried again after you failed? Give an example.

_____

_____

_____

Verse for the Day

I do not regard myself as having laid hold of it yet; but one thing I do: forgetting what lies behind and reaching forward to what lies ahead, I press on toward the goal for the prize of the upward call of God in Christ Jesus. (Phil. 3:13–14)

UpWords

There is courage housed in your faith. Use it and your faith will seize the day! As you trust the promises of God, forgive yourself, master your fears, and get back up.

S. Todd Townsend

Prayer

Lord, help me forgive myself when I've tried and failed, when I've fallen and haven't been eager to get back up. Put that *upward* call of God from Christ in me.

My Get-Up Response and Prayer List

_____

_____

_____

_____

After the Fall

(Refer to chapter 1 in *Getting Up from Being Down,* "The Get-Back-Up Hook.")

AFTER I FELL OUT OF a tree as a fifteen-year-old, it took me more than a year to climb another. I guess you could say it took me twelve months to get back up, although my injured arm was healed and back to normal many months prior.

Have you fallen in such a way that left scars and a residual fear that is keeping you from trying to get back up, get ahead, and move forward?

Describe an incident—a fall—that comes to mind that has adversely affected your life.

_____

_____

_____

_____

_____

What are the words *the fall* used to describe in Genesis 3?

_____

_____

What did this fall in Genesis 3 have to do with Adam and Eve's fellowship with God?

_____

_____

_____

Make no mistake, Adam and Eve had consequences for their disobedience. Read Genesis 3:16–24.

What were Eve's consequences?

_____

_____

What were Adam's consequences?

_____

_____

Notice in verse 21 that God "made garments of skin for Adam and his wife, and clothed them." This tells us that God made provision for Adam and Eve through the shedding of blood and is a foreshadowing of the death of Christ, who covered our sins on the cross.

The mandate of every human being is to get back up, whether we fall down physically, financially, emotionally, educationally, rationally, or spiritually. Whether we want to or not, whether we feel like it or not, there's a built-in mandate to get back up.

Often, after slowing down and being still, we feel the quiet voice of God deep down on the inside whispering to our hearts to get back up. But the devil will try everything in his power to get you and me to ignore God.

Describe a circumstance when you felt cut off from God because of something you did.

_____

_____

_____

Do you normally use your built-in mandate to get back up when you experience a fall?

_____

_____

You don't have to stay down. God has placed a divine trigger, a hunger in our souls, an instinctive yearning and need to get back up, no matter how bad the fall.

Verse for the Day

It was for freedom that Christ set us free; therefore keep standing firm and do not be subject again to a yoke of slavery. (Gal. 5:1)

UpWords

Remember, the productive usage of your liberty in Christ is the best evidence that God has recovered your life from bondage. Arise and shine!

S. Todd Townsend

Prayer

Lord, in areas of my life that are fallen, places that I have not submitted to You, will You help me to rise and stand firm today?

My Get-Up Response and Prayer List

_____

_____

_____

_____

Because He Lives

(Refer to chapter 2, "Christ Got Up from Being Down.")

MY GIVEN NAME, STACEY, MEANS *resurrection*. When I found myself pastoring a church called the Resurrection Center, I was amazed. Resurrection and getting back up as a way of life are imbedded in me—my personal brand.

What I mean by this is that God calls you and me by name. And that name becomes a brand. It's a prophetic tool. When used right, it's a very powerful influencer in our lives and the lives of others.

For instance, Abraham's name means *father of many nations*. Paul later describes him as the father of faith (Rom. 4:11–12, 16). The Jews called him "father Abraham" (John 8:53, 56). His brand worked.

Deborah's name means *bee*, so as an Old Testament prophetess and judge of Israel, I guess you could say she was a "Queen Bee." Her brand worked.

Moses's name means *drawn out*. It's not strange that while Moses succeeded in getting the children of Israel out of Egypt, he failed to get them into the Promised Land. Getting them out fulfilled his calling and destiny. His brand worked. Getting them in was someone else's job.

My job is to get back up again and bring others too. What about you?

What is the personal brand or a recurring theme in your life? (It could be reclamation, overcoming, survival, healing, etc.)

_____

_____

When you look back on your life, in what ways do you see God weaving a *get-back-up* pattern in all the different threads of your life?

_____

_____

_____

A golden thread of getting back up runs through the books of the Bible. Jesus Christ demonstrated this thread in His resurrection. Christ refused to allow any force of men, demons, or circumstances to keep Him down. Although He went down—way down—He refused to stay down.

To get back up, we need resolute determination, follow-through, and resolve.

Share a time when you needed determination to get back up after being down.

_____

_____

Do you normally follow through and take the steps necessary to get back up, or do you sink into a giving-up pattern?

_____

_____

Is your will lined up with God's will today?

_____

_____

Verse for the Day

I am the resurrection and the life; he who believes in Me will live even if he dies, and everyone who lives and believes in Me will never die. Do you believe this? (John 11:25–26)

UpWords

Mapped by destiny, labeled by circumstance, and honored with a new name from above, the champion in you emerges to win against the odds. With each battle along the way, your victories are named, recorded, and installed into your legacy. Rise up now; adorn that which is granted by the grace of God—and live!

S. Todd Townsend

Prayer

Lord, infuse me with resurrection life and give me the resolute determination to follow through with the steps You have placed before me today.

My Get-Up Response and Prayer List

_____

_____

_____

_____

Do You Have What it Takes?

(Refer to chapter 2, "Christ Got Up from Being Down.")

GOD HAS EQUIPPED US AS warriors with spiritual weapons for *every* battle, *every* trial. That equipment is called the armor of God. Ephesians 6:11–17 tells us to "put on the full armor of God." Let's consider how to do that.

What do you think the belt of truth is (v. 14)?

_____

_____

How does the breastplate of righteousness cover our hearts (v. 14)?

_____

_____

Ephesians 6:15 says we are to put on our feet the "preparation of the gospel of peace."

How does that relate to sharing the gospel?

_____

_____

_____

What are some ways faith shields us?

_____

_____

Obviously, a helmet is worn to protect the head. That speaks to me of how we are to guard our minds and thoughts. God gives us a weapon to accomplish this—His peace: "And the peace of God, which surpasses all comprehension, will guard your hearts and your minds in Christ Jesus" (Phil. 4:7).

Describe an experience when you were in a situation where you unexplainably had God's peace.

_____

_____

_____

How should being a Christ follower affect your thought life?

_____

_____

_____

Isaiah 59:17 says of God, "He put on righteousness like a breastplate, and a helmet of salvation on His head." This tells me that these are pieces of *God's* armor that He gives us. You do have what it takes! Now this time, say it out loud: "I do have what it takes!"

Jesus Christ got up from being down. He got up from the dead. He is the quintessential model of victorious living. Instead of settling down on the downside of death, He turned His circumstances around and ascended to the upside of life. He is the source of our getting-up power. We can tap into the power of Christ's resurrection in our daily lives.

Verse for the Day

Finally, be strong in the Lord and in the strength of His might. Put on the full armor of God, so that you will be able to stand firm against the schemes of the devil. (Eph. 6:10–11)

UpWords

Armor is the tool of the redeemed. Armor well used honors the skilled warrior. Purpose in your heart to stand in the presence of your enemies fully armed and assured of victory!

S. Todd Townsend

Prayer

Lord, help me to look to You as my source. Keep me safe from the negative forces of men and women, demons and devils. Help me to depend on Your armor in whatever circumstances come my way today.

My Get-Up Response and Prayer List

_____

_____

_____

Life Is So Daily!

(Refer to chapter 3, "Getting Up Daily.")

I GREW UP IN A dangerous inner-city context. On the streets where I hung out, the flow of talk was ugly with hopelessness. At home, my stepfather imposed his appetite for violence on my mother and me. Although we had fun together, my stepbrother would also regularly beat me up on his weekend visits. On the following Monday mornings, I'd have to get back up and move forward.

I also have memories of my mom's strong endurance through the many storms in our lives. No matter how many times she was knocked down, she'd get back up.

Everyday life can be an ongoing season of paradox. Life's challenges and life's obstacles must be managed. We handle both the beautiful and the difficult simultaneously. We don't surrender, fall back, or quit. Neither do we perpetuate a spirit of doubt or readily give in to temptations.

Moment by moment, no matter what happens, in my thinking, my values, daily responsibilities, and communications, I'm raising the standard, and I'm getting back up.

Getting back up daily is a spiritual weapon, an instrument of redemption, a powerful tool!

Let's talk about the things that get us down in our daily lives.

How do you handle discouraging thoughts? Are you tempted to hang on to them and live surrounded by them, or can you release them and give them to God? Give an example.

_____

_____

_____

What circumstances tend to get you down in your life?

_____

_____

_____

There are times when we all want to evade or escape our responsibilities. How do you deal with the sameness of the tasks or responsibilities you have?

_____

_____

What inspires you to get back up daily?

_____

Verse for the Day

And He has said to me, "My grace is sufficient for you, for power is perfected in weakness." Most gladly, therefore, I will rather boast about my weaknesses, so that the power of Christ may dwell in me. Therefore I am well content with weaknesses, with insults, with distresses, with persecutions, with difficulties, for Christ's sake; for when I am weak, then I am strong. (2 Cor. 12:9–10)

UpWords

Each new day adorns itself with unique opportunities to rise again. Harness the moments and waste none!

S. Todd Townsend

Prayer

Lord, I need Your grace. Exchange my weakness for Your strength today.

My Get-Up Response and Prayer List

_____

_____

_____

_____

Down for the Count?

(Refer to chapter 3, "Getting Up Daily.")

THE LINEMAN FROM THE OPPOSING team hit me so hard it knocked me down and took my breath away. I looked up at him standing over me, grunting like a grizzly and smiling, and lay back down on the ground. I was down for the count, and the coach didn't put me in any more games. Back in high school, I didn't want to put in the necessary effort to be a winner; I just wanted the trophy. I took a shortcut. It was a hard way to learn one of my most important lessons in life: shortcuts take too long.

Small daily moments can hold us in bondage if we don't get back up. Consistent patterns of small failures to get back up can defeat God's purposes for us.

In 2 Timothy 2:5, Paul says, "If anyone competes as an athlete, he does not win the prize unless he competes according to the rules." No shortcuts!

In that football game, I didn't obey the get-back-up rule.

Were there shortcuts in your youth you wish you hadn't taken?

_____

_____

In your career or job, were there shortcuts you took that didn't help you? Were they worth it?

_____

_____

_____

What did Moses do to take matters into his own hands and try to bring about change when he saw one of his people being beaten? (See Acts 7:22–30.)

_____

_____

How many years of preparation did Moses undergo when he was hiding in the wilderness in Midian? (See Acts 7:29–30.)

_____

At eighty, Moses was prepared and fully equipped to get back up and be God's vehicle for redemption and deliverance.

What parts of your life do you feel God was preparing you for what He had in store?

_____

_____

_____

The foundation God builds under us gets us ready for the impossible in our lives, lifts us out of a negative mindset, and renews a right way of thinking.

In what stage of construction is your life?

Foundation building? _____

Ready for action? _____

Full potential? _____

The stage I am in in my life is:

_____

_____

Verse for the Day

By faith Moses, when he had grown up, refused to be called the son of Pharaoh's daughter, choosing rather to endure ill-treatment with the people of God than to enjoy the passing pleasures of sin, considering the reproach of Christ greater riches than the treasures of Egypt; for he was looking to the reward. By faith he left Egypt, not fearing the wrath of the king; for he endured, as seeing Him who is unseen. (Heb. 11:24–27)

UpWords

If you hesitate, you may give occasion to peril or birth to danger. So choose the option of action—faith-filled and obedient action!

S. Todd Townsend

Prayer

When I am tempted to take a shortcut or a zigzag or not to get back up and back in the game, strengthen me, Lord.

My Get-Up Response and Prayer List

_____

_____

_____

_____

A Rough and Rocky Journey

(Refer to chapter 4, "Getting Up for the Journey" and 5, "Getting Up from the Past.")

THE ROAD I'VE TRAVELED ON my journey was rough and rocky. I was a criminal, a rabble-rouser, a car thief, and a home robber—nothing more than a common thug. For twenty-three years, I didn't believe in God because I'd never seen Him working for me. As a kid, my life wasn't filled with awe and wonder; it was drugs and hustling, beatings and brutality. Trapped on the outside, miserable on the inside, and living an ungodly life in every way just to survive, I had no idea how to change the trajectory of my life.

Though I was surrounded by destructive behavior, it's obvious to me now that God built a defense against it as high as the walls of Jericho. And He gave me a gutsy mama who was the strength of my existence. But when I'd think about the word *father* when I was a child, I felt the pain of my real father's absence and my stepfather's abuse.

What association does the word *father* bring up for you?

Neglected	_____	Accepted	_____
Rejected	_____	Loved	_____
Forgotten	_____	Remembered	_____
Abused	_____	Protected	_____

God can take the pain and shame of the past and transform it into strength. He took my pain and my fatherless void, my rejection and neglect, and created my caring and compassion for the fatherless. He used my past to get me up for the journey ahead.

In what ways has destructive behavior been a part of your past?

_____

_____

If so, what gave you hope that your situation could be different?

_____

_____

Who in your life exhibited the love of Father God to you?

_____

_____

Verse for the Day

A father of the fatherless and a judge for the widows, is God in His holy habitation. God makes a home for the lonely; He leads out the prisoners into prosperity, only the rebellious dwell in a parched land. (Ps. 68:5–6)

UpWords

Let the mistakes of your past become the strategic building blocks of your future. By so doing, you wisely exchange your former debts for future prosperity.

S. Todd Townsend

Prayer

Would You pour Your love into my empty places and give me hope where I feel hopeless?

My Get-Up Response and Prayer List

_____

_____

_____

_____

New Day, New Way

(Refer to chapter 6, "Getting Up and Walking the Walk.")

TO GET OUT OF A downward lifestyle, we must walk straight down a narrow path.

Jesus Christ said, "Enter through the narrow gate; for the gate is wide and the way is broad that leads to destruction, and there are many who enter through it. For the gate is small and the way is narrow that leads to life, and there are few who find it" (Matt. 7:13–14).

The good news is that we don't have to change ourselves to walk that narrow path—God makes us new. He renews our minds when we yield our lives to Him and accept Christ's death on the cross as the perfect sacrifice to atone for our sins.

How you live matters! If you've ever thought you can continue in your downward and sinful pattern because God's grace will cover you, listen to what Paul says in Romans 6:1–2: "What shall we say then? Are we to continue in sin so that grace may increase? May it never be! How shall we who died to sin still live in it?"

As born-again believers in Christ, we are *alive in God*, not dead in sin. Rather, we are dead *to* sin. The redemptive power of God working through Christ makes us new.

Through willed obedience to our heavenly Father's command, we rise up again and again and again.

In your life, what are some of your wide-gate places or situations?

_____

_____

_____

What are some of the narrow-gate choices you've made that have led to abundant life?

_____

_____

_____

Verse for the Day

And do not be conformed to this world, but be transformed by the renewing of your mind, that you may prove what the will of God is, that which is good and acceptable and perfect. (Rom. 12:2)

UpWords

Take intentional steps without procrastination toward the new you. Momentum begets distance; distance covered demonstrates new possibilities and broadens your range; an expanded range motivates new visions of self!

S. Todd Townsend

Prayer

Thank You, Savior, for making me new. Renew my thoughts so I can fully obey You and walk into the new things You have for me today.

My Get-Up Response and Prayer List

_____

_____

_____

_____

This Pilgrim's Progress

(Refer to chapter 6, "Getting Up and Walking the Walk.")

HAVE YOU HEARD ABOUT THE guy who goes on this epic journey to get rid of the heavy load he was carrying? Yes, I'm talking about John Bunyan's classic, *Pilgrim's Progress*. In this allegory, Christian, the main character, journeys from where he lives, the city of Destruction, toward his destination, the Celestial City. He's desperate to get rid of the unbearable burden he carries on his back. On his journey, Christian meets Evangelist, who tells him to seek out a shining light and a gate where he will find deliverance.

On the way, Christian falls into the Slough of Despond where doubts, lusts, temptations, and sins sink him down into the boggy swamp. Christian survives the swamp but encounters other seemingly insurmountable challenges. At every step along the way, he meets with resistance.

Like Christian, we must be authentic in our walk of faith, step out of the swamp of our temptations and fears, overcome our own obstacles, and walk out into this glorious newness.

What fears or temptations are you dealing with or need to overcome?

_____

_____

_____

There's no more dramatic example of such a transformation than the moment a person gives his life over to Jesus Christ.

I'll never forget watching that glorious moment when my mom saw all her sins washed away. Until that moment, she had no idea she was beautiful, loved, and forgiven. In that moment, she realized that God's ultimate victory over a life of condemnation was undeniable. Through Christ, she saw she could transition from the old to the new.

Describe that point in your life when you knew you were made new, when Christ had transformed your thinking and started you off on a new path—the path of obedience to Him.

_____

_____

_____

Who in your life are you praying for to meet Christ as their Savior and Lord?

_____

_____

Verse for the Day

Therefore if anyone is in Christ, he is a new creature; the old things passed away; behold, new things have come. (2 Cor. 5:17)

UpWords

My new me . . . has forgotten my old ways!

S. Todd Townsend

Prayer

Thank You, Lord, for granting mercy for my account and qualifying me for service. I transfer my burdens to You and cast all my cares on You because you care for me.

My Get-Up Response and Prayer List

_____

_____

_____

_____

Facing the Giants

(Refer to chapter 6, "Getting Up and Walking the Walk.")

WHEN I WAS A CHILD, the violence, screaming arguments, and perverse language of my stepfather became the tools he used to control my mother and me. I had no hope of rising out of this oppression. My only thought was escape, but it seemed hopeless.

I tried to defeat the Goliath in my own life with my mouth shut instead of getting up and boldly learning to walk the walk.

David was probably just a teenager when he stepped out—overcame apathy—and used what was in his arsenal to defeat a giant of a man.

For most people, overcoming stagnation and mediocrity is the hardest step they will take.

Describe a time when you had to step out in faith to defeat a giant in your life.

_____

_____

_____

There is a way to overcome resistance and step up in the battle against the giants in your life. You can take that first bold step to *get up*. Transform that scary step into a path of power by breaking down any overwhelming task into smaller chunks and achievable goals.

The battle can be won by seeking *small victories*.

David didn't defeat Goliath in one stroke. His victory came in small steps, one decision at a time.

What are some small victories—small steps—you have taken toward facing your giants?

_____

_____

_____

_____

Are you ready to transition from loser to winner?

In what areas do you need victory in your life?

_____

_____

What are some changes you know you can you make yourself?

_____

_____

_____

_____

What behavior pattern do you need to address to soar spiritually?

_____

_____

Verse for the Day

For this is the love of God, that we keep His commandments; and His commandments are not burdensome. For whatever is born of God overcomes the world; and this is the victory that has overcome the world—our faith. (1 John 5:3–4)

UpWords

Our matriculation through the university of adversity produces a degree of faith in our walk with God that overcomes the world . . . one victory at a time.

S. Todd Townsend

Prayer

Father, thank You for the victories You have in store for me as I exercise my faith and step out in obedience to You!

My Get-Up Response and Prayer List

_____

_____

_____

_____

Think on These Things

(Refer to chapter 7, "Getting Up from a Down Lifestyle.")

IN MY NEIGHBORHOOD, THERE WERE plenty of negative people who were ever ready to do damage to someone or something. Not all the people were like that, but these were the circles I traveled in. These negative relational circles fed into us a defeated sense of hopelessness about the future. These feelings led to mental patterns of reluctance and resistance about getting an education and working hard to get ahead. Such hopelessness led to a narrowed peripheral vision and a downward lifestyle with a variety of destructive selections as the only options.

To be free from the shackles of that down lifestyle, I had to have a change of mind. I had to think right. I had to reject the mindset of failure, doubt, and impossibility. In order to see that I could rise up in life beyond what I thought were my limits, I needed my down thinking renewed.

Our minds can defeat us if our thoughts are fighting against each other. It's called being "double-minded," and yes, that means to think two different ways. James 1:8 refers to a "double-minded man, unstable in all his ways."

To think right and live right, we must keep our minds on the right things. The Bible teaches the power of upward thinking. Here's some help from Scripture:

Finally, brethren, whatever is true, whatever is honorable, whatever is right, whatever is pure, whatever is lovely, whatever is of good repute, if there is any excellence and if anything worthy of praise, dwell on these things. (Phil. 4:8)

Set your mind on the things above, not on the things that are on earth. (Col. 3:2)

For as he thinks within himself, so he is. (Prov. 23:7)

It's important to hide God's Word in your heart, to actually read the Bible for yourself rather than just listen to someone tell you about it.

What strongholds of thinking do you hide behind (fear, despair, hopelessness, cynicism, pornography, etc.)?

_____

_____

_____

Are there areas of hopelessness in your sphere of influence or circumstances that affect your vision for the future? Please describe.

_____

_____

_____

What are some ways that work best for you to hide God's Word in your heart?

_____

_____

How do you handle impure thoughts or when you are tempted to look at things that encourage impure thoughts?

_____

_____

_____

Verse for the Day

And do not be conformed to this world, but be transformed by the renewing of your mind, so that you may prove what the will of God is, that which is good and acceptable and perfect. (Rom. 12:2)

UpWords

Rich quality in my thought life will fuel and inform my standard of behavior.
Pure cleansing of my thought life uncovers facets of God-given brilliance.
True power in my thought life will govern well my daily course.
The limitless potential of my thought life can change the world.

S. Todd Townsend

Prayer

Father, renew my mind today as I practice thinking true, honorable, right, and pure thoughts.

My Get-Up Response and Prayer List

_____

_____

_____

_____

Escaping a Roach-Box Mentality

(Refer to chapter 7, "Getting Up from a Down Lifestyle.")

AS A CHILD, THE SHADOW of darkness was cast on me beyond my power to control. As a teenager, I began to create my own shadow. Trapped in a home saturated with pain, in a neighborhood wet with violence and surrounded by friends swimming in criminal behavior, my environment defined the lens through which I saw life. I was overshadowed by fear and swimming in what I call a roach-box mentality. Let me explain.

You know the little roach boxes you place under sinks in places where roaches live—the boxes where the insect gets stuck and can't get out? All the bug can see is the confines of that dark prison.

Jesus Christ offers an escape from the roach-box mentality. He says, "I am the way, and the truth, and the life; no one comes to the Father but through Me" (John 14:6).

His way is forgiveness. He forgives us as we forgive each other. "And forgive us our debts, as we also have forgiven our debtors" (Matt. 6:12).

Don't let the shadow of your past define your future. Ask God to change you. Ask Him to help you see clearly and replace that roach-box view with a positive perception about life.

Here are some ways to be free:

1. Do some spiritual housecleaning.
2. Let go of the wounds of your old down lifestyle.
3. Cast off the old.
4. Gather people around you who can help you.
5. Hold on to new principles, thought patterns, behaviors, and new values.

What areas of your mind and soul need spiritual housecleaning?

_____

_____

Are there wounds from your old life that have built up scar tissue that keeps you from moving freely? Describe.

_____

_____

_____

Why do you think it is important to have people around you who can help you walk in freedom?

_____

_____

Name those who help you grow rather than tear you down.

_____

_____

_____

How does your old thinking affect your getting-up behavior?

_____

_____

_____

Verse for the Day

Set your mind on the things above, not on the things that are on earth. (Col. 3:2)

UpWords

Untamed fears from the past multiply, becoming rodents of doubt scouring about the soul. If they are not exterminated quickly, they permeate the heart much like an infectious disease that pollutes future hopes.

S. Todd Townsend

Prayer

Lord, cleanse me from the inside out. Help me to let go of my wounded places so I can walk freely in Your truth. Redirect my thoughts toward You and bring those around me who will help me grow.

My Get-Up Response and Prayer List

_____

_____

_____

_____

The Heavenly Endurance Contest

(Refer to chapter 8, "Getting Up and Enduring.")

OUR ABILITY TO RUN OUR race well, to sustain success, and to heal our damaged lives relies on endurance. According to *Merriam-Webster's Collegiate Dictionary*, *endurance* means "the ability to withstand hardship or adversity; the ability to sustain a prolonged stressful effort or activity."

I'm often forced to wrestle with my own battles to endure. For me, it was family pain, the darkened street life, and criminal behavior that shaped and developed both my reputation and my outlook in life. Believing in my own bad reputation fed me false notions of myself and created an outlook that crafted dishonest expectations—expectations of quick and easy gratification.

I had to learn the lessons of endurance and wait patiently for my change to come, even when I didn't fully understand when that change might come or what that change would be.

How does a street guy—a criminal—change and become a preacher? The answer: God's grace! Paul said it this way, "But where sin increased, grace abounded all the more" (Rom. 5:20). And abound it did. God mercifully snatched me from a depressed worldview, transformed my soul, and lifted me to higher ground. There's more.

After my radical transformation by Jesus, my lessons in endurance were far from over. I had to learn to endure accusations from my past. I had to deal with people focusing on what I used to be and the things I no longer did. I heard, "You're a street guy—a criminal." Those negative words were designed to block me from becoming what God wanted me to be. But my new born-again friends erased my appetite for my old criminal friendships.

What negative labels did others give you when you first came out of your old life?

_____

_____

What relationships in your life are holding you back?

_____

_____

_____

What relationships in your life are strengthening your resolve to live for Christ?

_____

_____

Running to God, instead of running from God, wasn't easy. Yet, God's truth began to resonate in my head when He said, "My son, if sinners entice you, do not consent" (Prov. 1:10).

Alcohol, drugs, and violence had perverted me, beaten me, and eclipsed all I could do. I had lost my sense of who I really was because of my misplaced priorities and misguided preferences. I had to realize that the new me, the new nature, the saved person, didn't belong in those old places, and he didn't belong with those old things. If I stayed there, they would eventually eclipse the light God wanted to give me—the light I could become.

I had to learn what Christ did for me. He died and rose again to offer us eternal life so that we might enjoy our lives in abundance and to the fullest.

Have you struggled with alcohol or drug abuse or the effects of a violent lifestyle? What helped you? Are there areas in which you still need to persevere toward deliverance?

_____

_____

_____

Verse for the Day

Blessed is a man who perseveres under trial; for once he has been approved, he will receive the crown of life which the Lord has promised to those who love Him. (James 1:12)

UpWords

As a soldier in the Getting-Up Army of the Lord, I have no contract with ease and comfort, no charter exemption from trials and troubles, and no pass from life's appointed difficulties. What I do have is endurance! What I will have is reward!

S. Todd Townsend

Prayer

Lord, thank You for dying for my sins. When I feel like giving up, help me persevere and raise me to new heights with You. I'm looking for You to show up powerfully in my life.

My Get-Up Response and Prayer List

_____

_____

_____

_____

Get Up and Stay Up

(Refer to chapter 8, "Getting Up and Enduring.")

DO YOU WANT TO KNOW the will of God in your life? Getting up and staying up is the will of God for you!

It's kind of like boxing.

When Joe Frazier knocked down Muhammad Ali in a boxing match, Ali, who usually knocked his opponents out, didn't stay down. In their next two fights, he came back to win. Being down doesn't mean the fight is over. Good fighters find a way to get back up.

Christ was victorious over death, hell, and the grave, and He now makes intercession for us. Because Christ got up from the lower parts of the earth after His death, we as believers are likewise vested with His great getting-up resurrection power. That power is an authority over things low, an authority laced with the enduring ability to get up. That power motivates us and gives us the drive to get up.

Jesus knows our down setting even better than we do ourselves. He understands all our infirmities and inabilities to identify, address, and conquer the downward pull. He understands this because He has been tested and tempted at all points familiar to our existence in a fallen world as fallen beings, yet He did not sin. He is interceding for us now.

Because of Christ, being down is no longer a justifiable basis for staying down.

Where are the low spots in your life?

_____

_____

_____

How do you typically handle negative occurrences in your life?

_____

_____

_____

Do you often experience depression?

_____

_____

_____

Verse for the Day

For we do not have a high priest who cannot sympathize with our weaknesses, but One who has been tempted in all things as we are, yet without sin. (Heb. 4:15)

UpWords

In review,
as I look back,
it becomes clear . . .
I gained my best strengths during my worst events.
I owe my greatest gains to my biggest losses.
I gained my strongest muscles during my heaviest encounters.
I owe my best genius to my most confusing circumstances
. . . and I gained eternal *life* through His timely *death*.

S. Todd Townsend

Prayer

Lord Jesus, You know everything about me. You know when I'm down and when I need lifting up. Lord, fill every part of my being with Your resurrection life so I can truly live.

My Get-Up Response and Prayer List

_____

_____

_____

_____

Vision Matters

(Refer to chapter 8, "Getting Up and Enduring.")

HAVE YOU EXPERIENCED THE DEATH of something you felt was a vision for the future? I have.

The Bible tells us about the three cycles of a vision—the birth of a vision, the death of a vision, and the fulfillment of a vision. Before our visions can come to pass, something must die. It's like the seed that must die in the ground before a plant can sprout up.

Joseph had a dream. In Genesis 37 we read about his dream of his brother's sheaves of wheat bowing down to him, as well as the sun, moon, and stars.

Joseph probably wasn't wise when he told his brothers, "Your sheaves bow down to mine." They already hated him because their father, Israel, had a special multi-colored tunic made for him, and hearing about that dream made them hate him more. Then he told his brothers and his mom and dad, "The sun, the moon, and eleven stars were bowing down to me." That didn't go over very well either.

Jealous, his brothers called him a dreamer and threw him in a pit, intending to kill him. But after one brother pleaded his case, they sold him off to some traders passing by.

Joseph didn't know it, but he was about to go from a pit to a prison. When you're in a pit, that's the death of a vision, and his vision seemed dead.

In Genesis 39–45, we read how the vision was fulfilled by Joseph becoming a ruler of Egypt and saving his family and the Israelites from dying of starvation in the famine that came on the land. When Joseph's brothers finally fell down before him, he told them not to be afraid, saying, "As for you, you meant evil against me, but God meant it for good in order to bring about this present result, to preserve many people alive" (Gen. 50:20). The vision was fulfilled.

Don't lose hope; what God has promised, He will bring to pass.

Describe a vision/dream of yours that died.

_____

_____

_____

Has that dream been resurrected and fulfilled? How?

_____

_____

_____

Describe a time when it felt as if your circumstances were falling apart, but God brought about good in spite of the circumstances.

_____

_____

_____

Verse for the Day

And we know that God causes all things to work together for good to those who love God, to those who are called according to His purpose. (Rom. 8:28)

UpWords

God is Creator. He installed us in the Creation . . . and placed within us the Creative. You are, therefore, an artistic visionary by design with only the horizon for a limitation. Unveil your internal eyes . . . and dream beyond your external condition.

S. Todd Townsend

Prayer

Lord, You are always good, and Your purposes in my life are good. Help me to surrender my dreams, my circumstances, and my life to You so You can make of them what you will. Today I choose to thank You for the hard things and look for the fulfillment of Your promises to me.

My Get-Up Response and Prayer List

_____

_____

_____

_____

Shifting into Gear

(Refer to chapter 9, "Getting Up and Engaging the Drive.")

GOD HAS A CLARION CALL on your life to fulfill your destiny. To fulfill this call, you'll have to engage the inner drive He placed in you. This inner drive is a holy, supernatural drive. I call it an overdrive.

The *Oxford Living Dictionary* defines the noun *overdrive* as:

> A gear in a motor vehicle providing a gear ratio higher than that of the drive gear or top gear, so that engine speed and fuel consumption are reduced in highway travel; a state of high or excessive activity; a mechanism that permits a higher than normal operating level in a piece of equipment, such as the amplifier of an electric guitar.

In other words, we need to get it in gear to get going.

Like it or not, there's a war going on. Satan has launched this war against God's people, and we need His overdrive to rise up. All of us have a call to rise up, to go up, to not permit Satan to gain ground in our lives.

Describe the type of call God has on your life.

_____

_____

Engaging this drive means remaining positive in your mind, no matter the circumstances, and trusting the Lord, no matter what happens.

What areas of your life are difficult to be positive about?

_____

_____

_____

What circumstances are hardest for you to trust God for?

_____

_____

_____

What is one specific area you need God's help in trusting Him for today?

_____

_____

When challenged to rise up and follow God's leading into something new, what excuses do you fall back on?

_____

_____

_____

How has the shame of your past kept you from responding to God's upward call?

_____

_____

_____

Verse for the Day

From the end of the earth I call to You when my heart is faint; lead me to the rock that is higher than I. (Ps. 61:2)

UpWords

When summoned, go readily! Simply heed the call and shift. Change gears with swift elegance and smooth resolve. Repeat this action as a daily pattern of obedience to heighten performance.

S. Todd Townsend

Prayer

Lord, when I am afraid to go higher, lead me. Fill me with Your Spirit and Your presence so I can rise up and fulfill Your call on my life.

My Get-Up Response and Prayer List

_____

_____

_____

_____

Temptation and You

(Refer to chapter 9, "Getting Up and Engaging the Drive.")

TEMPTATION COMES TO EVERY ONE of us with its promise of fast results and a quick fix.

In my younger life, the temptation to get fast money was my perpetual downfall. I watched my stepdad do it, and it affected me, even though I hated his behavior. The devil knew that my temptation to secure easy money could work because I had seen it in motion.

Being tempted is not sin, but yielding to temptation is. It's easy to get pulled into temptation, into doing what you know is wrong, because the temptation promises some sort of positive outcome.

What was God's command to Adam in Genesis 2:16–17?

_____

_____

_____

In Genesis 3:1–5, what temptation did Satan use to entice Eve?

_____

_____

_____

Satan directed Eve's temptation away from the thousands of trees in the garden they had access to, focused it on the forbidden one, and made them think they were missing out. Have you ever felt God is holding things back from you? Has that been a temptation for you to take matters into your own hands to achieve a desired outcome? Describe.

_____

_____

_____

_____

Yielding to temptation can jeopardize your future. The downward pull of temptation tries to keep you from fulfilling God's calling on your life. But God has a way out. He calls it a "way of escape." Watch for the way of escape to keep on *getting up*!

Verse for the Day

No temptation has overtaken you but such as is common to man; and God is faithful, who will not allow you to be tempted beyond what you are able, but with the temptation will provide the way of escape also, so that you will be able to endure it. (1 Cor. 10:13)

UpWords

Authentic humility is a key deterrent to the devil's temptations in our lives. Had such humility been at work in the garden of Eden, Adam may not have lost paradise so quickly. So, as Christ did when he was tempted for forty days in the wilderness, let us choose submission over disobedience as God's way of escape, thus defeating temptation's power.

S. Todd Townsend

Prayer

Lord, when I am tempted, show me the way of escape You have provided so I can endure it. Thank You for Your faithfulness in my life to make a way for me.

My Get-Up Response and Prayer List

_____

_____

_____

_____

Wake Up and Live Right

(Refer to chapter 10, "Getting Up and Waking Up.")

WE MUST WAKE UP BEFORE we can walk up. But we can't do this on our own. We need a divine "waking up"—an awakening in our souls and lives. The Spirit of God wants to stir an awakened determination in our spirits. This divine waking up compels us to get up from being down.

Are you discouraged or feeling down?

- Come to a knowledge of God's truth.
- Instead of thinking negatively, look for the good God is working in your life.
- Expect the good.

Write down three good things God is working right now in your life.

1. _____
2. _____
3. _____

What three areas of your life are you asking God to do something good in?

1. _____

2. _____

3. _____

Since "the righteous man shall live by faith" (Gal. 3:11), we need to deny our fear and display our faith.

What fears would you like to be rid of today?

_____

_____

_____

Dare to believe the glory of the Lord will rise upon *you*!

Verse for the Day

Arise, shine; for your light has come, and the glory of the Lord has risen upon you. (Isa. 60:1)

UpWords

Now beloved, step up into the light as do kings and queens with a public performance of self-mastery. Conquer your imbalance with the weapons of integrity, and torch hesitation in the fires of confidence.

Walk!

Walk upright!

Walk before God!

S. Todd Townsend

Prayer

Lord, awaken my heart so I can respond to Your upward call in faith. Help me to watch for You in my circumstances with the eyes of faith and not of fear.

My Get-Up Response and Prayer List

_____

_____

_____

_____

Wake Up and Come To

(Refer to chapter 10, "Getting Up and Waking Up.")

REMEMBER THE PARABLE OF THE prodigal son that Jesus told? A young man insulted his father by asking for his inheritance while the father was still alive. He left the family home and squandered his estate on loose living. When there was a famine in the country, he was reduced to the low-down job of feeding pigs and wasn't given food for himself—not even pig food.

When he was starving and living surrounded by pig waste, he "came to himself" and decided to return to his father and the provision of his father's house. The Prodigal had a wake-up moment.

When I realized my life did not have to be defined by my circumstances or my difficulties, it triggered a glorious wake-up moment in me.

We all need to come to the realization that we need the Lord. God wakes us up out of ignorance of who we are—and awakens us to who He means us to be. We find we are unique in our purpose, we have more to offer than we thought, and life in His will has more to offer than we ever dreamed.

In Luke 15:11–32, what was the Prodigal's wake-up moment?

_____

_____

How did his father react to his coming home?

_____

_____

How did his brother react to his father blessing him?

_____

_____

How do the loving and accepting actions of the father in the Prodigal's story match up with your experience with your earthly father or father figure?

_____

_____

_____

How has your picture of what Father God is like been affected by your earthly father figure?

_____

_____

Ask God to make His love real to you. Let Him welcome you home, as the Prodigal's father welcomed him.

Verse for the Day

Furthermore, we had earthly fathers to discipline us, and we respected them; shall we not much rather be subject to the Father of spirits, and live? (Heb. 12:9)

UpWords

Internal insights working from within work their way out. Eating pig's food can provoke much needed insight. When you finally see your own prodigal tendencies and wake up, at that very moment *get back up* and go back home . . . to your rightful inheritance. Your Father is waiting.

S. Todd Townsend

Prayer

Father God, make Your love real to me today. Show me Your Father's heart for me so I can rise up into Your loving acceptance and the inheritance You have for me.

My Get-Up Response and Prayer List

_____

_____

_____

_____

Who Am I?

(Refer to chapter 10, "Getting Up and Waking Up.")

EVER FACED A WHO-AM-I MOMENT?

Moses sure did. He was hiding out on the "backside of the desert" when God got his attention in a big way. He turned to see a bush in flames, which was no big deal; but when the bush didn't burn itself up, it was a big deal!

God often uses unusual occurrences to make us sit up and notice before He speaks to us.

Next, Moses heard God speaking to him out of the burning bush. He called him by name, and Moses answered Him, "Here I am."

Then God spoke instructions for a task He wanted Moses to do—a giant task that involved getting two million people out of Egypt when the ruling pharaoh didn't want to let them go—a humanly impossible task.

Faced with this task, Moses answered, "Who am I?" Was he looking at his past failure? Was he thinking of the impossibility of the task? One thing he *wasn't* thinking about was the greatness of God. God is much bigger than our pasts and our failures.

Has God ever tasked you with something you thought impossible? Or are you facing such a circumstance now? Please explain.

_____

_____

_____

After he asked, "Who am I?" God showed Moses His supernatural power. He had a personal interaction with God and experienced the power of God, and then he was ready to obey God. Moses found out who he was when he partnered with God and allowed God's power to work through him.

Have you had a personal interaction with God? Describe.

_____

_____

_____

Tell some instances when you experienced the power of God (healing, intervention, provision, etc.).

_____

_____

_____

_____

Is there something in your life that God has asked you to do that you are struggling with? Please describe.

_____

_____

_____

Verse for the Day

Looking at them, Jesus said, "With people it is impossible, but not with God; for all things are possible with God." (Mark 10:27)

UpWords

There is little in life that can withstand one's clear sense of identity and self-command. Humbly partner your knowledge of self with God's great "I Am," and you, my friend, will rise to see mountains skip like lambs and oceans part before you.

S. Todd Townsend

Prayer

Lord, I want to hear Your voice speaking into my life as I face impossible circumstances. Show me Your power and work through me as I partner with You.

My Get-Up Response and Prayer List

_____

_____

_____

_____

Follow in My Steps

(Refer to chapter 11, "Getting Up and Being Trained.")

FOR YEARS, I MISTAKENLY THOUGHT I could do everything on my own. But I was blessed to have people who believed in me when I didn't even believe in myself. To mature, each of us needs the source of inspiration and support system that a godly mentor can bring. We need the help of others to bring to pass the future blessings God has planned for us.

There are four categories of uniquely-gifted, God-given individuals we need: role models, mentors, peers, and partners.

In my life, I needed someone whose steps I could follow. Pastor Reed became one of my first role models. He was there in the first years of my walk with the Lord when I was hungry for the Word.

Role models are those whose behavior we imitate. Of course, Jesus should be our first role model. He said, "I am the Light of the world; he who follows Me will not walk in the darkness, but will have the Light of life" (John 8:12).

There's an element of sacrifice in following the steps of Jesus. He said, "If anyone wishes to come after Me, he must deny himself, and take up his cross and follow Me" (Mark 8:34).

What elements of darkness in your life has your relationship with Jesus shined a light on?

_____

_____

_____

What does it mean to you to "deny yourself" and "take up your cross"? Give examples.

_____

_____

_____

The apostle Paul said, "Be imitators of me, just as I also am of Christ" (1 Cor. 11:1). Who were some of the early role models in your life as a Christian?

_____

_____

_____

_____

What qualities in your mentors have you imitated?

_____

_____

_____

Are you mentoring another person?

_____

Verse for the Day

Sanctify them in the truth; Your word is truth. As You sent Me into the world, I also have sent them into the world. For their sakes I sanctify Myself, that they themselves also may be sanctified in truth. (John 17:17–19)

UpWords

I gain important insights about what God wants to accomplish in my life and a telling visual of what that looks like by paying close attention to who God sends to train me.

S. Todd Townsend

Prayer

Lord, thank You for those you have brought into my life as role models. Thank You for being the ultimate role model. Teach me to deny myself and take up my cross and follow You today.

My Get-Up Response and Prayer List

_____

_____

_____

_____

Mentoring for Growth

(Refer to chapter 11, "Getting Up and Being Trained.")

FINDING THE RIGHT MENTOR DID wonders for my personal life and character development. Pop Carrington's example and ethics crept into my family values and behavioral patterns; his heart for ministry still beats in my ministry performance today. His influence in my life as a mentor cannot be overstated. As a new Christian and young adult, I finally experienced a safe, constructive environment and a taste of loving and caring fatherhood. Without his mentoring and the leadership of others who followed and gave me advice and guidance, I would have been lost. Instead, because of them, my talents and abilities were nurtured and provided fertile ground from which to blossom.

All of us are looking for opportunities to be a part of something—to belong. A mentoring relationship fulfills that need for belonging and connection and promotes growth.

The Bible is full of mentoring relationships; in fact, mentoring seems to be the pattern for growth. In the Old Testament, we see Jethro mentoring Moses, Moses mentoring Joshua, and Eli mentoring Samuel, to name a few. In the New Testament, Jesus mentored the apostles, the apostles mentored many, including Paul, Paul mentored Titus and Timothy, and Priscilla and Aquila mentored Apollos.

Who in your life have been your godly father or mother figures who spoke into your life and have helped you grow?

_____

_____

_____

What specific qualities did they have that influenced your life?

_____

_____

_____

Jethro, Moses's father-in-law, counseled him to appoint judges to preside over minor disputes, while Moses would only judge the difficult disputes so he didn't wear himself out. (See Exodus 18:5–27.)

What are some life skills you have learned from a mentor that have positively influenced your life?

_____

_____

_____

_____

Whether we know it or not, our lives are mentoring others—for good or ill. Ask God to make you aware of those whose lives you are influencing and for sufficient grace to walk uprightly.

Verse for the Day

Do nothing from selfishness or empty conceit, but with humility of mind regard one another as more important than yourselves; do not *merely* look out for your own personal interests, but also for the interests of others. (Phil. 2:3–4)

UpWords

Don't be the person who cannot be advised. Let wise counsel find you daily, and you will rise as a wise mentor who blesses others with good counsel.

S. Todd Townsend

Prayer

Father God, thank You for those You have brought into my life to help me grow. Help me encourage someone else today for the kingdom's sake.

My Get-Up Response and Prayer List

_____

_____

_____

_____

The Right Kind of Peer Pressure

(Refer to chapter 11, "Getting Up and Being Trained.")

PEER PRESSURE OFTEN HAS A bad reputation. But the affirming pressure of another with the same goals as you can be great peer pressure. Peers are just contemporaries at the same stage of development. A peer makes you bring your best to the table.

The best peer relationships are where both parties keep everything real. The greatest reward is watching your peer grow to their greater call, their greater purpose, as you continue moving upward and growing yourself.

Among others, my friend Steve Kamal challenges, motivates, encourages, and inspires me as we do life and ministry together as we have occasion.

David and Jonathan in the Old Testament were friends who loved each other with a godly love and had each other's backs.

What does 1 Samuel 18:1 say about David and Jonathan's friendship?

_____

_____

_____

How did Jonathan show his practical regard for David's needs in 1 Samuel 18:4?

_____

_____

How did David and Jonathan express their covenant of friendship in 1 Samuel 20:42?

_____

_____

_____

In the New Testament, Paul, Timothy, and Epaphroditus were loyal friends who were co-workers and took care of those close to them.

How did Paul describe the role his coworker Epaphroditus plays in his life (Phil. 2:25)?

_____

_____

_____

Value the people God brings into your life as godly peers. We are stronger when we stand together!

Verse for the Day

Iron sharpens iron, so one man sharpens another. (Prov. 27:17)

UpWords

Faithful wounds from a faithful friend are a far better corrective than the deceptive praises of an enemy. Such wounds excite correction and improvement without leaving scars.

S. Todd Townsend

Prayer

Lord, help me build up others in my peer relationships, not tear them down. Thank You, Jesus for Your example of humbling Yourself when You were here on earth. Keep me from rivalry and competition and help me be united in spirit with the people You have brought into my life for Your good purposes.

My Get-Up Response and Prayer List

_____

_____

_____

_____

Learning to Be One Flesh

(Refer to chapter 11, "Getting Up and Being Trained.")

IN OUR MARITAL PARTNERSHIP, CLEO and I have traveled thirty years of successful fidelity, friendship, education, ministry, parenting, and leadership. It has all been built on the biblical principle found in Genesis 2:24: "For this reason a man shall leave his father and his mother, and be joined to his wife; and they shall become one flesh."

We adopted this "one-flesh" vision as our core marital value and mission. We graduated together with our PhDs; we are the first husband and wife pastors in the 126-year history of our church; we've taught courses together, conducted marriage counseling sessions and workshops together, and even taught fitness classes and ride motorcycles together.

God defined our lives, our partnership, as *together*—as one.

Our partnership is built around our relationship with the Lord. He is the glue, the "tie that binds," that keeps our relationship strong. The Bible says, "A cord of three strands is not quickly torn apart" (Eccl. 4:12).

We see an example of such a marital partnership in the relationship of Priscilla and Aquila (Acts 18:2, 26). True partners, their names are always mentioned together. They worked together in the making of tents. They taught the Word of God together, often in their home, and traveled together in spreading the gospel.

Letha Scanzoni, in a groundbreaking 1968 article, "Elevate Marriage to Partnership" in *Eternity* magazine wrote, "Two made one *In Christ* should be able to experience a depth of sharing, a richness of companionship, and a unity of purpose unknown to those who have never "tasted and seen that the Lord is good."

If married, what challenges have you found in maintaining a healthy one-flesh relationship?

_____

_____

_____

_____

"Marriage is to be held in honor among all," says Hebrews 13:4.

In what ways do you honor your spouse in your marriage?

_____

_____

_____

Verse for the Day

For this reason a man shall leave his father and his mother, and be joined to his wife; and they shall become one flesh. And the man and his wife were both naked and were not ashamed. (Gen. 2:24–25)

UpWords

In its full expression and relentless blossom, *marital oneness* is undeniable, incontrovertible, undefeatable, incontestable, unquestionable, and indisputable. Though often underestimated, it remains eternally irrefutable, indubitable, and definite!

S. Todd Townsend

Prayer

Lord, thank You for instituting marriage as a one-flesh relationship. Teach me how I can serve and not just be served; teach me to honor and love wholeheartedly, using all the fruit of the Spirit.

My Get-Up Response and Prayer List

_____

_____

_____

_____

Becoming a Trainer

(Refer to chapter 11, "Getting Up and Being Trained.")

WHETHER YOU KNOW IT OR not, you are being trained to be a trainer.

The successful outcome of our getting up and being trained is that we become trainers ourselves. As former trainees, the mantle of trainer is passed to us. As trainers, we must grow all over again. We grow as we move from being information consumers to being information providers, from being life-lesson receivers to life-lesson givers. In other words, the act of training others is, in itself, training us. The trainer grows sharper and becomes more astute as a result of training others, which is God's way of keeping the trained . . . in training.

Training others is called making disciples, and it's something all Christians are commanded to do. In Matthew 28:19–20, Jesus said, "Go therefore and make disciples of all the nations, baptizing them in the name of the Father and the Son and the Holy Spirit, teaching them to observe all that I commanded you; and lo, I am with you always, even to the end of the age." A disciple is "one who accepts and assists in spreading the doctrines of another," according to *Merriam-Webster's Collegiate Dictionary*.

Our followers become a reflection of our lives. This new group of learners and followers affirms our growth and transformation from follower to leader. The apostle Paul said, "If to others I am not an apostle, at least I am to you; for you are the seal of my apostleship in the Lord" (1 Cor. 9:2). Paul was simply saying that his reflection within them was the seal of their growth and his authenticity.

The process of making disciples is one of God's proven ways of training the trainer.

How did Paul express being trained in 1 Corinthians 9:27?

_____

_____

_____

What role does personal discipline play in the lives of those who train others?

_____

_____

_____

Is personal discipline something you struggle with? Give examples.

_____

_____

_____

Verse for the Day

To the weak I became weak, that I might win the weak; I have become all things to all men, so that I may by all means save some. I do all things for the sake of the gospel, so that I may become a fellow partaker of it. (1 Cor. 9:22–23)

UpWords

Celebrate! Then applaud the privilege, the invitation, the calling, sent from God Himself to you and me to become ambassadors and kingdom representatives to the world. Then—simply *go*!

S. Todd Townsend

Prayer

Lord, thank You that You promised to be with us as we make disciples. Open my eyes to the people You are bringing into my life, and help me to be obedient to share Your Word, Your gospel, and my life with them.

My Get-Up Response and Prayer List

_____

_____

_____

_____

Facing Fear with Faith

(Refer to chapter 12, "Getting Up by Believing.")

YOU GOTTA BELIEVE!

If you place yourself on the altar of God's truth and embrace your God-given identity, He will lift you up and free you from your insecurities, self-doubts, overstressed relationships, toxic emotions, and even your fears of lack from living paycheck to paycheck. Nothing will stop you, no matter what trials you face in life.

It's about forgetting the bad stuff that happened to you yesterday—but also forgetting yesterday's victory and looking for a new one.

It's all about the power of faith. Believing leads to bold actions. By believing in the power of God's Word, our bold actions create bold results.

Fear is normal, but it must be met with faith. Face the fear and balance it with God-given direction. Go scared, but go anyway!

I have found it helps to fight fear when I have a goal sheet where I write my personal vision and goals on 3 x 5 cards and meditate on them in the evening at bedtime and first thing in the morning.

Write your personal vision and goals for the immediate days and for the future. What are your relationship goals, financial goals, and spiritual goals?

_____

_____

_____

I have also found it helps to have a life verse—a verse that speaks to your core and gives you inspiration, hope, and strength.

Write your life verse here:

_____

_____

_____

If you don't have a life verse, ask God to give you one; then listen and watch for Him to do so.

Noah overcame his fear when God asked him to do something incomprehensible—build an ark when it had never even rained before on earth (Gen. 6).

Has there been a time when you moved forward in obedience to God in fear, even when you didn't understand? Please describe.

_____

_____

_____

_____

Instead of being immobilized by fear, use that fear to move into God's power. Move past your fear, and trust God to release His mighty power to work in your life. Don't worry. Don't fret. Don't fear.

Believe.

Verse for the Day

The Lord is the one who goes ahead of you; He will be with you. He will not fail you or forsake you. Do not fear or be dismayed. (Deut. 31:8)

UpWords

Faith releases your true wingspan. And it does so in the face of your fears. So, move on up to higher altitudes one flap, one flight, two wings at a time.

S. Todd Townsend

Prayer

Lord, I give my fear to You and ask that You strengthen my faith as I move forward in obedience today to what You are asking of me, even when I don't understand.

My Get-Up Response and Prayer List

_____

_____

_____

_____

Soaring in Newness of Life

(Refer to chapter 13, "Getting Up and Becoming New.")

I WAS TRAPPED IN THE pit of sin until Christ came low to bring me high. I was rescued by the Master's hand, lifted from patterns and habits of sinking down to patterns and habits of soaring up.

On September 16, 1984, God saved me and called me as I prayed and confessed with my mouth that I believed in my heart that God had raised Christ from the dead after He had suffered and died for me. Since that wonderful day, I have walked with Christ and grown in and by His grace. Being born again is the best thing that has ever happened to me on earth.

If you have been born again, tell your conversion story here.

_____

_____

_____

_____

If you are not certain that you have been born again, you can know beyond the shadow of a doubt today. Confess your sin and acknowledge Christ as your Savior and Lord. God's Word in Romans 10:9 says, "That if you confess with your mouth Jesus as Lord, and believe in your heart that God raised Him from the dead, you will be saved."

God not only rescued me from the penalty and power of sin, but He placed a holy calling in my heart. He takes us the way we are and makes us into something new.

Becoming new, being born again, is walking in newness of life. We step out of our past mistakes, our lost opportunities, out of a low place, a pit, and become brand new. We are lifted up to the heights of God's grace and seated in heavenly places in His providential purposes for us.

God, the Master Potter, shapes and molds us through the trials He allows in our lives.

Share a trial in your life that molded your character.

_____

_____

_____

_____

What verse or verses have been meaningful to you as you face life's trials?

_____

_____

_____

Verse for the Day

Therefore if anyone is in Christ, he is a new creature; the old things passed away; behold, new things have come. (2 Cor. 5:17)

UpWords

Real change, like flowing water, gives evidence to real life—nothing remains still. At its core, being born again, represents much more—the best possible change that can occur in one's lifetime. It is most refreshing!

S. Todd Townsend

Prayer

Father God, thank You for sending Your Son to be my Savior; thank You for saving me and making me new. Help me keep my eyes on You today, despite my circumstances, as I learn to soar in the heavenlies.

My Get-Up Response and Prayer List

_____

_____

_____

_____

Rising to Serve

(Refer to chapter 14, "Getting Up to Serve.")

THE DIFFERENCE BETWEEN WHO I was and who I am now is like night and day. The contrasts that separate my family of origin and my immediate family dynamics are staggering, as well as the contrasts between my former and current professional activity. God lifted me from a place of abusive rejection to a place of eternal and loving affirmation. Without the Lord saving me, I would have simply replicated the behavior of an abuser I saw patterned.

When God saved my soul, He renewed my mind and made me a giver, not a taker. I have been chosen and elect to live as a humble servant to my wife, my children, my family, my church, and the community, as opposed to being an oppressive, abusive ruler.

What were the patterns and dynamics of your family of origin?

_____

_____

_____

A Christ-centered family with its biblical boundaries results in emotional, spiritual, physical, social, and mental health for family members.

What positive results have you seen from following biblical principles in your own family?

_____

_____

_____

What areas of your family life or family members are you believing God to work in?

_____

_____

_____

To make serving God a priority in our lives, we need to turn from serving sin. The person who serves sin is a slave to sin.

What does Romans 6:23 say will be the result of serving sin?

_____

_____

Self-sacrifice is at the core of service in God's kingdom. Serving God is a lifestyle, not a short-term temporary position. It involves a decision to do so. Service is inevitable if you want to maximize your relationship with God.

What does 1 Timothy 3:13 say are the results of serving well?

_____

_____

List your experiences in serving the Lord.

_____

_____

_____

_____

How has serving grown and matured your faith?

_____

_____

Serving is perhaps the most meaningful gift you can give back to God. I love serving! I absolutely love serving the call of Christ that is upon my life. This love affair with God was ignited over thirty years ago, and the fire only burns more brilliantly today.

In what areas would you like to serve the Lord in which you are not presently doing so?

_____

_____

Ask the Lord to open doors for you; then begin by serving in a small way, not caring who gets the credit.

Verse for the Day

Knowing that from the Lord you will receive the reward of the inheritance. It is the Lord Christ whom you serve. (Col. 3:24)

UpWords

I have not worked hard for the Lord to make myself known or look good; to the contrary, I labor hard to serve well. For if I do well in good works, He—my Father—is glorified.

S. Todd Townsend

Prayer

Thank You, Lord, for all You have done for me and all the good gifts You have given me. I choose this day to serve You out of gratitude and love. Work in me to do Your good will and that which pleases You.

My Get-Up Response and Prayer List

_____

_____

_____

_____

Up, Up, and Away!

(Refer to chapter 15, "Getting Up and Staying Up.")

GETTING UP AND *STAYING UP* is an offensive, not defensive, action, an aggressive kingdom action. It's fighting for what God has promised you and taking back territory. It's not letting the enemy stop you from your God-breathed destiny in life. It's taking the risks. It's reaping the rewards.

If you get up and then *stay* up, you are being repositioned from a downward lifestyle to a life of fulfillment, a life on fire for God, a life of prosperity and greatness.

We all face the daily challenges of everyday life—relationships, work, finances, family, and marriage.

Marriage can be an up-and-down ride for many. If you are hitting a low point, get back up, stay up, and keep climbing. Far too many marriages wind up in divorce court, many times over financial issues that complicate the relationships. Money management can definitely be a roller-coaster ride. We need to stay up, keep moving forward in faith, and not go backward.

How have financial struggles or the inability to get ahead had a negative influence on your marriage or family?

_____

_____

_____

Part of growing in faith is learning to trust God for our marriage or family relationships and our finances. I can testify that God has been faithful to us. Though we have had many moments where we lacked the dollars to pay bills or invest in opportunities, God has taught us to get our expectations up by faith and not by sight.

Galatians 2:20 tells us how we are to live: "I have been crucified with Christ; and it is no longer I who live, but Christ lives in me; and the life which I now live in the flesh I live by faith in the Son of God, who loved me and gave Himself up for me."

Do you see it? We are to live by faith in the Son of God.

We don't have to do this life on our own.

We don't have to struggle alone in our relationships or with our finances.

We do it by faith in our all-powerful Savior and Lord who has called us out of darkness into His glorious light. He has promised to be with us to the end.

I'm counting on it!

What are you believing God for today?

_____

_____

_____

_____

Verse for the Day

For I know whom I have believed and I am convinced that He is able to guard what I have entrusted to Him until that day. (2 Tim. 1:12)

UpWords

We must! We can! We do! We will ascend our personal mountains while scaling life's most difficult moments and whirlwind issues. Up is the call! Up is the journey! Up is the challenge! Up is the destination!

S. Todd Townsend

Prayer

Lord, I put my trust in You once again; I declare You are Lord over my life, my relationships, my family, my finances, and my future. I want to rise, stand, and stay standing by faith in the One who loved me and gave Himself for me.

My Get-Up Response and Prayer List

_____

_____

_____

_____

The Golden Thread

YOU'RE PROBABLY VERY AWARE BY now of what I call the essential golden thread that runs through this book. That thread is the consistent call to *you* to "Arise, shine; for your light [and time] has come" (Isa. 60:1). In other words, it's time to get up!

I trust that after spending these six weeks with the book and workbook, you are no longer the same. You may have been intimidated by doubt, shame, or emotional pain and suffering. You may have led your life as if God didn't exist or care about you.

My prayer is that you have learned step-by-step to get back up in your life and stay up, that you are walking by faith and are intimately acquainted with God's peace and presence.

What lessons in this study have caused you to grow in your faith?

_____

_____

_____

_____

You've learned about my troubled past in a violent home and on the mean streets of Philadelphia. That golden thread of getting back up in life ran through even the darkest parts of my past, is running through my present, and will run on into my future.

Your life and your past may be worse or far better than mine. Yet there is a golden thread running through your life as well, or you wouldn't be reading this.

We fall down, yes. And we will fall down again. But no matter how many times we fall, we can get back up.

Getting back up is the power God's given us to transform our lives.

What are some of the instances when the thread of getting back up was evident in your life?

_____

_____

_____

_____

We've also learned that our call is to *stay up*.

There is unimaginable reward in staying up. By doing so, we rebuild our lives and learn to be people of integrity. Our behavior lines up with what we believe as the power of Christ shines through us.

The awakening of our getting-up power becomes a guiding force in our lives, calling us to step out of our comfort zones and ascend to our own unique God-directed paths.

As you get up and stay up, may your faith be strengthened and your legacy transformed.

The call of God is an invitation to come up . . . get up . . . go up . . . to shine! As a result, we will reap crowns and benefits.

But before we wear the crown, we first must run the race. God be with you as you rise, shine, and run for Him!

Verse for the Day

Therefore, since we have so great a cloud of witnesses surrounding us, let us also lay aside every encumbrance and the sin which so easily entangles us, and let us run with endurance the race that is set before us. (Heb. 12:1)

UpWords

As a skilled artisan, the wisdom of God enriches the golden thread of life . . . one stitch at a time within you. He patiently embroiders passionate works of art within the gallery of your heart and the museum of your soul—all for others to behold.

S. Todd Townsend

Prayer

Thank You, Lord, for calling me out of my fallen ways to come up higher, to rise in newness of life and shine for You. Make my life all You want it to be as I follow You, seek Your face, and listen for Your voice today.

My Get-Up Response and Prayer List

_____

_____

_____

_____

Order Information

To order additional copies of this book, please visit
www.redemption-press.com.
Also available on Amazon.com and BarnesandNoble.com
Or by calling toll-free 1-844-2REDEEM.

CPSIA information can be obtained
at www.ICGtesting.com
Printed in the USA
FSHW011444020419